Empower Your Dog for a Thriving Life

Empower Your Dog for a Thriving Life

How you can Fulfill the Basic Needs for Greater Success with Your Dog

Jane Madigan GDMI

Carl,

Enjoy the 'moments'
with Biggie & Puffy!

Love

Jane xo

2019 Jane Madigan GDMI

All rights reserved.

ISBN-13: 9781794050624

Dedication

FOR MY LOVELY WILLOW – ALWAYS REMEMERED

Table of Contents

Acknowledgements

With deep appreciation and thanks to my wonderful friend Barb Bowie, whose belief and encouragement gave me the courage to write this book. Her editing skills and advice are a constant inspiration.

Thank you to all the dogs that I have been fortunate to work with, in showing me what they needed to be successful and to show me patience while I learned from them.

A special thanks to Bud, who always brings me into the moment with laughter and a bark!

Introduction

In any relationship, getting to know the other person is all about them feeling comfortable with you and developing trust and safety. This will take time depending on where they have been and how life has treated them.

It is the same for your dog. They need to get to know you, as the person who is going to care for them, be in their life, and for them to be part of a family.

You need to know who your dog is, how they learn and who they are before you can start any specific training that you need to do. Then you can decide what you would like to help them with to become the best of themselves.

When you begin the right way, which is ensuring your dog's basic needs are met consistently, their character and who they are will start to shine through. With this basis of trust and safety being developed, your relationship will start to form into a deep and compassionate understanding of fun and friendship.

We are privileged in that we can share our lives with each other and show unconditional love and companionship.

These basic needs have been modified over two decades of reading, research and putting into action, "The Basic Needs for Success". Whether working with guide dogs in their kennel environment or working environment and the many rescues I have had the pleasure of working with, one thing has become abundantly clear, when you apply the basic needs you will see who in essence the dog is. At this point you are supporting them into being the best of themselves

Basic Needs

"Your dog's basic needs, when fulfilled in the right order, will allow for thriving and success to take place at both ends of the leash"

Your dogs' character is based on breed specifics and genetics. The experiences of their life up to the point when you take them into your life has a bearing on how they will cope and deal with situations.

Their behaviour issues or baggage will arise after a short time with you. You will see your dog for who they are based upon breed, genetics and the life they have lived so far.

Being able to assess your dog and support them through this transition period with you, by ensuring their basic needs are met, will give you the information you need to support them on their journey to a thriving life.

As you go through the levels and the aspects of trust and safety are established and maintained, your dog will start to look to you for support, especially in times of need.

Thoughtful, kind and compassionate training will help in their overall development.

However, when your dog goes into a new situation or environment and no consistency from you is maintained, then your dog will go back to previous learned behaviours.

Consistency with the basic needs, in any environment you and your dog go into, is paramount in ensuring success with the development of two of the most important aspects of the relationship – Trust and Safety.

Human Needs

Before I talk about how to fulfill your dog's needs, let's see how a human's needs have to be consistently fulfilled before we can learn and thrive in any environment.

The basic needs for survival are well known and are a natural requirement for every living being. How we act, think, live and cope with life in general in any one moment is based on these needs, that are constantly being fulfilled as we enter new environments. Once the needs are met with consistency, a persons' survival can transform to a learning and thriving state.

The problems start to show themselves in our behaviour when the basics are not met. Becoming short tempered, irritable and unable to deal with what life sends our way are just some of the things that can be expected. Surviving becomes our focus and understanding and learning become jeopardized because we are stuck in a survival state.

When you are in a situation of learning a new task, such as being in a new town or city, a new environment, etc., your basic needs have a habit of showing themselves to you. Your needs of water and food are suddenly on your agenda. Your brain is sending signals to every cell in your body "where is water, where can I find food, what type of shelter is there?" Think about it. What situation have you been in where you are trying to learn something and all you can think about is food and your need to quench your thirst? This is true for me, as an example, when I go to a new city and stay in a hotel for a conference, my life and safety needs present themselves.

My Needs

Let me explain… arriving at a new city, I drive myself to the hotel. I am nervous about driving, new signs, street names and trying to remember where to go (after checking a map). I don't use a GPS as I can't focus on the voice telling me where to go. I have to focus on driving and knowing where I am going. The drivers around me seem to be in a hurry, they know where they are going so it is second nature to them. I arrive at my destination.

Once I have found where to park, I check in and introduce myself to the person at the check-in desk, who I hope is nice. I look around, taking it all in, noticing nearby landmarks, where things are located in the lobby. I get to my room and check to see if there is tea and coffee available … yes! Good! I then check the bathroom… nice, clean, fresh towels. Then I check how soft the bed is on my way to look out the window and get my bearings. When I see the hotel folder with information telling me when meals can be served, when the restaurant is open, what the wi-fi password is and general hotel logistics, I feel more comfortable. All of this information helps me to feel safer. Knowing that I can make my own hot drink without having to leave the room allows me to feel comfortable and safe, then my anxiety starts to lessen.

Once settled and refreshed, I venture out to find which room the conference is in and the information that I require to be in a state of learning. I find the information on a board in the lobby and go to the conference to register and meet people. Once there I am given a schedule of the day's events. Guess what I look for? What time does it start and finish? When the breaks are, when will refreshments be provided and how long is each presentation? What are the seating arrangements? Where will I sit and my need to be near an exit or window (as a personal preference).

All of the information I need has been provided to me for my survival at the conference, then once I am in the room and listening and watching the presentations, I am able to focus and learn.

My success while at this event can only be achieved when the other needs for survival are fulfilled. I cannot go without refreshments or bathroom breaks to feel comfortable in a new learning experience. It will just not happen. I will not achieve anything, my body will be screaming at me to fulfill my food and water intake, etc. I will be fidgety and distracted.

Guess what?... your dogs are no different. They need you to supply, maintain and nurture these needs so they are in a place of thriving.

It is so true for your dog. Fulfilling and maintaining these needs transforms them to a healthy relationship built on trust and safety.

Let me show you how the basic needs of success work. In the diagram "The Basic Needs for Stepping into Success" you will see I have outlined the levels and what each level consists of.

Each chapter explains how to fulfill each level. I can show you how your dog will build up their relationship with you as you go through and maintain these steps, in any environment you take them into. You will see a clearer picture of who, in essence your dog is.

The diagram is set out in steps. As you progress, they will merge together in your daily life and become a natural habit and thought process.

Your awareness to your dogs' needs, will influence their transition to the next level.

With reaching each level, your dog goes towards a successful learning state. If a need is not being met, they will go back a level (as seen in behaviour issues).

The Basic Needs for Stepping into Success

Learning
A Learning State
for Success

Achievement
Feeling Good
Trust

Belonging
Family, Affection
Group Dynamics

Safety
Security, Guidelines
Order and Limits

Life Needs
Food, Water, Shelter,
Warmth, Sleep

Our awareness to the dogs' needs, will influence their transition to the next level.

With reaching the next level, the dog goes toward a successful learning state.

If a need is not being met, they will go back a level.

Jane E Madigan

Willow's Story

"We cannot change the essence of who the dog is. However, we can transform them into being the best of themselves"

The first 24 hours

Willow came into my life when she was 16 months old. I was working as a Guide Dog Instructor at the time and she was one of the new intakes that was assigned to me.

This is the start of her story. Getting to know each other, seeing how she was in the moment, who in essence she was so I could support her on this new chapter in her life.

Kennels

The Puppy Walking Supervisor brought her from her puppy walker into the kennels. I met them both as they got out of the car and we took Willow into a free run area to relieve herself, move around and have a good sniff and look around. Once she had 20 minutes to "just be" and with me kneeling down so she could approach me, when she wanted to, our relationship started.

When the supervisor left, Willow's behaviour changed. She started to whine and ran up and down the fence line after watching the car drive away. I moved around and every time Willow looked at me or came over to me, I reassured her that everything was fine. When she stood by me, I calmly stroked down her shoulder (the one nearest to me), with the back of my hand. After a short while she came and sat by me and leaned her body into mine. She made more eye contact and I returned her glances with soft eyes and licking my lips gently. She did the same back to me.

Attaching a leash to her collar, I took her into the kennel block and showed her into her assigned kennel. It was an 8' x 8' with a water bowl, bed and a privacy wall plus fencing so she could see her neighbours.

I busied myself with some paperwork while I stood a few feet away, watching her look and move around. There were other dogs coming and going with their trainers. The radio was on and I had set it to a low volume and made sure it was on a classical station (classical music has been scientifically proven to settle brain waves). Ref:1

Meeting Daisy

Willow had started to pant and pace with all of the movement that was happening. I supported her with my voice, waiting for the activity of the kennel to subside. Once it had, I went and got Daisy, one of my other dogs. She was established in her training and was a calming influence. I walked past Willow in her kennel, talking to her and Daisy who was on leash. When I spoke to one dog, I looked at her and vocally praised her before looking at the next dog and then praising her.

I put Daisy back in her kennel and went and got Willow. I then took her out to the free run area, where she first met me. I went and got Daisy and brought her into the free run area so both dogs could meet. I kept Daisy on a long leash and allowed both dogs to sniff each other. I called Daisy back to me after 5 seconds, so the intensity of any potential buildup lessened. I then allowed Daisy to move back towards Willow while saying "nicely girls, nicely" in a calm voice. After 10 seconds I called Daisy back to me and at the same time, as Daisy was turning away from Willow, Willow turned away from Daisy. Both had their heads lowered to the ground, both licking their lips, and I continued to praise "nice going girls."

I walked around slowly, Daisy still on leash, both sniffing the ground quietly. I slipped the long leash off of Daisy, still walking. They went running off, sniffing the ground and then peeing. Bringing in the words "Busy, Busy" as they peed and "Good girls, nicely" as they ran around and interacted nicely, was rewarding them vocally in the moment.

They ran around, interacting with each other and as the free run area was about 25' x 25' they could not build up too much speed or be too far away from me. I supported them with my voice "Nicely girls" and watched as I gained information about Willow from her interaction with Daisy.

I called them both to me and gave them some nice contact, each dog getting strokes with each hand. We remained walking around and interacting for 15-20 minutes before placing the leash on Willow and taking her back to her kennel. I went and collected Daisy and brought her into Willow's kennel, ensured there were three bones (always one or more than there were dogs) and sat down in the kennel with both of them, giving them calming strokes and supervising the bone chewing. After a short while both dogs were laying down and observing what was going on around them. At this point I exited the kennel and walked up the corridor, looking back and telling them they were doing an awesome job. They stood up and watched me walk away. I walked out of the kennel block, counted to 20, then came back in and walked past their kennel, occasionally looking towards them, watching their body language to gauge their comfort levels.

Willow was showing some concerns. Her pupils were dilated, her tail (although wagging), was tight and slightly lower than horizontal and moving fast. She was starting to pace and push past Daisy. Her panting increased as did the whining. Daisy was giving very clear calming signals to Willow, by looking away and moving onto one of the beds.

By this time the other trainers had returned with their dogs and I observed Willow while all this activity was going on. Her pacing, turning quickly in a circle and her panting had become quicker indicating her rising anxiety. All the extra activity and noise were adding to her concern.

I took her from the kennel and placed her in the kennel office, which was quieter and cooler. I stayed with her for about 20 minutes, helping her become calm with voice and touch and ensuring she had some cold fresh water which she could access.

Taking Willow home with me

I decided to take Willow home with me that evening. I fed her in the office once she had stopped the frantic panting. I thought she might gobble the meal so I placed a bone in her bowl to slow her eating, so she would not inhale it all at once. I anticipated correctly, and the bone slowed her down. Once finished, she took the bone and lay down on the floor to chew. I left her alone, checking in through the door's window that she was okay. She had settled, so I went about feeding and relieving my other dogs in the kennel block, in between checking in on her before taking her home for the evening.

Once in the car, I noticed she sat looking out the window, still panting. After the short drive home, I took her a short distance to where she would be relieving. She obliged when I asked calmly "busy busy" and then "good girl" once she had finished and came back to me.

Taking her upstairs to my apartment I kept her on a long leash as I showed her around. Her tail was very low and her movements were quick. I showed her into the kitchen and put fresh water in a bowl, placing it on the floor away from any foot traffic.

After half an hour of showing her the apartment I then made a cup of tea, unclipped the leash and she went off investigating again. At this point I was preparing a meal for myself. Willow would keep checking in with me, then move around the different rooms in the apartment continuously checking in.

She had discovered the toy box and had taken out all the toys and bones and scattered them on the living room floor!

I noticed her looking up at the ceiling fan (not turned on), lowering her body and backing away from it. She had not noticed it previously as her focus had been towards the toys on the floor. She backed herself out of the doorway, looking at the toys then looking up at the fan.

Observing how she was going through the concern over the fan gave me valuable information about who she was. I spoke to her calmly and reassured her "everything is fine Willow, I'll look after you."

I walked with her into the kitchen, then watched as she went back to pick up a toy. She looked at the fan as she stood in the doorway, panting, whining, fidgeting, head and tail low with eyes looking up. I quietly walked past her, picked up the nearest toy, speaking to her as I did, and gave her the toy. She took it gently from me and went and lay down in the kitchen for a few minutes and played with it. Then she was up again and pacing around the apartment.

Settling

Once I had my meal ready, I went into the living room and sat down on the sofa to eat. Willow was by this time venturing into the room with one eye on the fan and the other on the toys. While I tried to eat, Willow was constantly on the move. I called her and asked her to lie down on the dog bed I had placed by my feet. She could not be still. I could see her thinking about what to do next. Pacing in and out of the rooms, panting and whining.

I attached a leash to her collar and asked her to settle on her bed. Each time she got off I gently encouraged her back with the leash to the bed. Two seconds later she was on the move again. I maintained this for what seemed like hours but was really about half an hour. I remained consistent in what I was asking her to do, used "good girl" when she came back onto the bed, so she could figure out what I wanted her to achieve. When she moved away from the bed, I softly asked her with a gentle ease and release of the leash to come back to the bed. I allowed her the full range of the 7 ft. leash. She needed to move and the leash was never taut. No negative or force was used. The leash gave her a gentle boundary. The bed was where she needed to be. It was a guideline for her.

She eventually settled and laid on her bed. I gave her one of her toys and I sat holding one end of the leash, the rest was lying loose on the bed attached to her collar and I went back to finishing my now cold meal. She placed her head down, closed her eyes and fell asleep. She was out cold, exhausted by the day's activities. The noise of the knife and fork on the plate did not wake her. I stood up and sat down again. She did not move. She was in a deep, exhausted sleep.

I sat and waited for her to awaken. I looked at my watch, made a note of the time and 25 minutes later she suddenly woke up, got up and was on the move again. I kept her on her leash, took her to her water bowl to see if she needed a drink (she didn't) then took her outside to relieve.

She had a big pee, we went back in and I took the leash off and she continued her panting and pacing around the apartment.

She followed me everywhere when I moved, which is natural and expected when a dog is getting to know you and their new environment.

I sat down with her on the floor, next to her bed, while I watched some T.V. I held on to a smoked bone for her while she lay on her bed chewing. The chewing was hard and fast. I asked her to be gentle and when she was, I let go of the bone so she could have it. She seemed to enjoy this. She would stand up with the bone in her mouth and push it into me then run off with it, her tail wagging.

Bedtime

When it was time for bed, I took Willow out to relieve and walked halfway down the block and back. I was watching her responses to the new environment. Her head was on a swivel and I could see her anxiety starting to go up a notch.

Walking back to the house she started to slow her pace and sniff the lawns of the neighbours. I lived on a quiet street so there was not much car or foot traffic.

At night noise carries differently. Sounds become heightened and for a dog's night vision, they see movement better than us. Knowing this, our walk was short. Maybe 20 meters up the block before returning home.

Once Willow was in the apartment, she seemed more settled. Her pacing had slowed considerably and her panting, although still present, was slower and calmer.

She followed me, with toy in mouth, as I went about getting ready for bed.

I carried the dog bed I had used in the living room and placed it by my bed. A couple of toys came along too, which Willow thought was a great idea!

I showed Willow her bed as I sat on mine. She went on it and as she did, I said "on your bed" quietly and calmly. I was bringing in words to an action she was performing at the time.

If she went off her bed, I called her back and again, as she stood on her bed "on your bed" was said.

She settled for about five minutes then was up and back to the toy box, rummaging for a new toy! She came back and placed her toys and her front feet on her bed, "on your bed", "good girl". Then she was off and pacing around the bed, checking in on me.

I called her back, attached the leash to her collar and gave her the length of the leash to move around, just as I had done when I was eating my meal.

I knew both of us would not get much restful sleep that night. The important thing was to help her settle, give her some consistent guidelines as to what I was asking her to do and let her know this was a time of rest. And most importantly that she was doing a good job.

As the night progressed, she lay for longer periods on her bed. We both drifted off to sleep, both awakening when one of us moved to change position. I unclipped the leash. Willow checked on the toybox a few times, just to check no toys had gone walkabout! On her way back she had some water, then she came back to her bed and lay down "Awesome job, good girl" I said calmly and quietly. She took a large intake of breath, placed her head down and stayed there for the remainder of the night. It had taken her about 2 hours to reach this point. She had learned so much since we first met each other that afternoon. I was so happy that she was resting. It was a good sign.

Morning:

I knew I was being watched even before I opened my eyes! When I did, there was Willow's nose, two inches away from my face. Her head was moving in time to the wag of her tail, I started to laugh and talked to her. She was so happy I was awake and promptly gave me one of her toys! "Thank you, Willow!"

I took her down to the front door, placed the leash on her and we went back to the area where she had relieved the night before. "Busy, busy", she promptly peed, "Good girl" then I just waited to see if she wanted to poo too. She did. "Busy, Busy, good girl". I picked it up as she patiently waited on a loose leash, looking around her. "Thanks for waiting Willow, awesome job".

We went back to the apartment and once I had made a cup of tea, I fed her. The same routine as the night before, bone in the food and a drop of water to help aid digestion. As I placed the bowl on the floor, she watched every movement intently, however she made no attempt to go towards the bowl until I whistled, three short toots. (This is how we train the puppies to associate the whistle with food, so it is linked to recall). Then she ate her food. It was good to see that she ate slower this time and as before, took the bone out once she had finished and went off to the bedroom to chew on it.

Taking her back to the training centre in the car, she was more relaxed, no panting. Once we arrived back, I asked her to jump out, she just sat there looking at me! I waited for her to make a decision. Then she jumped out and quite happily walked with me to the training van.

Feeling Enclosed

Within the training van, crates were lined up, 4 along the side facing the side door and 4 placed directly on top. I opened the first crate, directly behind the drivers' seat. I placed a bone inside and called Willow up. She looked up and once she had calculated the 2 steps into the van, she jumped up. She stopped at the entrance to the crate. I leaned in and stroked her, telling her everything was good. Her tail was low and she was licking her lips constantly. She hesitantly took one step in and stopped. Sniffing the bottom of the crate, she stepped back out. I asked her if she was okay? She turned and jumped out of the van. As she did so, I went with her, loose leash, assessing why she was concerned with the crate, or was it the van itself.

I took her over to the free run area and let her have some off-leash time. I went and loaded my other training dogs from the kennels into the van, placing Daisy, the dog she had met the evening before, into the crate next to the one I was going to put Willow in.

I brought Willow back to the van, where she saw the other dogs waiting patiently, chewing on their bones. I called her up and she walked straight into the crate, turned around to face the door and picked up the bone, after saying Hi to Daisy. She lay down and I sat down near her and watched to ensure she was doing okay.

I closed the crate door. She immediately stood up and started to pant heavily. I opened the door and called her out and proceeded to take her out of the van and onto the grass. After a few moments of allowing her to look and sniff around, I took her into the kennels, so she could stay with the kennel staff, who would keep an eye on her, while I took my other training dogs out in the van to a local area to do there training. My decision not to take her with my other dogs was because I needed time with her to see if my thoughts on her finding enclosed spaces difficult, was valid.

Back at Kennels

When I returned at lunchtime, I asked how Willow was. The reports that came back were that she was unsettled in her kennel, panting and pacing. In the bigger relieving run and outside run she was less anxious. She did not like being left on her own but was more settled when the staff were close by and she could see them.

After lunch, I collected Daisy from kennels and put her in her crate in the van, then brought Willow outside. I was going to see if my thoughts of Willow not liking being enclosed were correct.

I wanted to see if I could put her in a crate above Daisy, so she could see out of the windows. After she placed her front feet up and onto the crate, I then gave her a leg up with her back legs. Once in, she turned around to face me, lay down and promptly started chewing the bone that I had placed in there, beforehand. I left the crate door open, while I took a step back to observe her. Then after about 30 seconds, I quietly closed the crate door. She remained calm.

I closed up the van and drove slowly around the training centre, watching her in the rear- view mirror. She remained lying down and chewing her bone, occasionally looking up and out the window.

After 5 minutes, I parked and went into the back to take her out. She was relatively calm, watching my every move. When I did open the crate door, I asked her 'wait', placed her collar and leash on, 'wait, good girl' then called her out. She hesitated, while she looked down to where she needed to place her feet. I told her she was doing a great job and there was no hurry. She looked at me, licked her lips, then looked down again.

"Okay Willow wait a moment and I'll give you a hand". I moved closer to the crate and crouched down so she could use my thighs as a step. She stepped down and once all four paws were on even ground, she wagged her tail and waited for me to take her out of the van. I told her she was awesome, and we went for a little walk to explore the centre and go into the offices.

She exhibited similar behaviour to how she was in my apartment. Curious but cautious, yet still moving with a quick gait, tail low and wagging fast. We went into the Instructors office and I sat down and helped her settle. She took a while, but she eventually did so.

Learning about who Willow was: In the 24 hours that I had spent with Willow, assessing her every step of the way, without asking too much from her, but showing her what I wanted, she had given me a great deal of information. This was just the start.

She was clear in how she was feeling. She had high anxiety, which kept building up into fidgety and panting behaviour when not supported into giving her something else to accomplish.

Her mental activity did not know when to calm or stop without my help. Her attention span was short.

Her coping mechanism was to fool around and play. She also chased her tail at great speed. I saw this in the morning once we had arrived at the centre and I put her in the grass run.

She had concern with the ceiling fan and loud noises.

Her gait was stiff, especially in her hind legs. On leash, she had learned to lean into the collar and pull.

She understood the 'Busy, Busy' command. Her poo was slightly loose (as expected being in a new environment).

She learned relatively quickly, when shown what was wanted of her. She also calmed and settled with a calm touch and voice.

She enjoyed human company and was good with another dog (who was calm and had good self-esteem).

She was funny and loved interacting with me and bringing me toys. Sometimes two at a time!

Over the next couple of days, doing the same routine and taking her home, she became more settled. Her anxiety was extreme as she was not able to cope with confined spaces or rooms where she could not see out, particularly when she was left alone.

She was not going to be a suitable candidate for guide dog training or any type of service/assistance dog. Her underlying and ongoing anxiety was a concern. She would need a home where she would be given constant guidance, consistency, patience, compassion and reassurance for her to thrive.

After some time of not being able to find the right home for her, I decided to adopt Willow. With the connection that we had, I knew she was the right dog for me. I knew we were meant to be together. It was one of the best choices I have ever made.

Jane E Madigan

Life Needs

"To thrive is to grow with unlimited possibilities. This is dependent on whether the survival needs are met consistently"

Life needs are the basic needs that are fundamental necessities for your dog. Going from surviving to a thriving life and then to a successful learning state.

How you go about delivering these basic requirements will give your dog an indication on who you are. And it will give you an insight into who your dog is.

Your dog's breeding, genetics, who their parents were (their genetics and upbringing) and your dog's own history, where they lived for the first weeks of their lives, where they have been (puppies, rescues, retired working dogs, service dogs) are all factors to who they are now, in this moment.

When you get your new dog, it is your responsibility to take care and nuture your dog to be happy and have a fun life with you.

Food & Water

These are the basic survival needs. Freedom to access clean, fresh water at all times. They do not have to ask for this, it is up to you to ensure they have water, wherever they are.

The water bowl must be in an area where your dog can easily access it. Clear of foot traffic, falling debris and in a quiet spot. Refresh twice a day. If your dog goes in a crate for any time, water must be provided in the crate.

Food is a basic need to survive. Watching your dog eat and how they eat, whether a quick or a slow eater, will give you the information you need on how they are feeling. As the days go by, he may start to relax. If he gobbles, place a Kong or bone in his bowl. This will slow him down and give him a chance to lick his bowl and slow down/calm his mouth action.

When feeding, it is important that once your dog starts to eat, move a couple of steps back, so you can watch them eat but also respectfully give them space, so they do not feel threatened. (A new dog will more likely be protective over food of any kind, because food is a life need.)

This is important. Why? Because this will avoid the necessity for your dog to show possessiveness with food.

I find feeding twice a day is a really healthy way for your dog to have the nutrients they need and the digestive system to work as it should with a complete meal. A healthy gut is a healthy dog.

If you give food treats at this stage, the dog will more than likely 'snatch' the food from you. Again, it is a life need. Showing and teaching them 'gentle' or 'nicely' should be done a few days into their life with you.

NO EXCUSE

This next point is one I feel very strongly about.

At meal times, you or anyone else does NOT have a right to take the dogs food away from them or place your hand into their food bowl, while they are eating.

There is no argument or excuse for doing so.

As a human example…. if you were in a restaurant eating a meal and someone came up to you and either put their hand in your food or took your plate away, while you were eating, what would you do?

How would you react?

Would you trust this person again?

How would you feel, eating your food if that same person stood over you, while you were trying to finish your meal?

Instinctive reaction survival mode is set off in the brain if there is any disturbance when you or your dog are eating.

Food is a basic survival need!

Relieving

Dogs are private creatures when it comes to relieving. They do not want to be stared at, rushed or hear over excited parents telling them over and over that they are so good!

Routine is so important and like humans they will relieve in what they know is a safe and familiar place.

To establish a routine, you have to be conscious of your dogs' needs and actions. They will indicate with their body language when they need to go. Fidgeting or looking for a quiet place, they may even go to the outside door. (Initially do not wait for a new dog to indicate that they need to relieve. They do not know you or your routines yet.). Do not wait for these actions but take them out every couple of hours, so they have an opportunity to go. Have a notebook handy, where you can record what time they go and if they do anything. As the days go by you will start to see a routine being established.

Action

Finding a safe, quiet area for them to relieve, whether on or off leash, is up to you. Privacy is paramount in the early stages. Allow them to sniff about, this might mean wind scenting (head up and nose pointing slightly upwards and twitching to catch the air scent), before they check out the ground. As your dog goes through the actions, squatting, lifting a leg or circling for a poo, bring in the words you will use to encourage them to go. I use "Busy, Busy", calmly and softly. When they are done, "Good girl or Good boy" again, calmly and softly.

They will associate the word with the action in time. Then each time you take them out and say

"Busy, Busy" they know that is what they are out there for.

Always, always go outside with them, no matter what the weather. Encourage them to relieve, pick up after them so the area is clean.

Actions to problems

Puppies/dogs that relieve inside rather than outside do so because they feel safer inside.

Areas that are too smelly and are used by many dogs will not necessarily encourage your dog to go. They may avoid those areas.

Watch body language. If your dog is concerned or uncomfortable (tail low or tucked between their back legs, stiff movement, head and eyes quickly looking about) they will not move away from you. If this happens walk slowly and quietly with them, in a 10-metre circle. This usually encourages them to move and they will, after looking around the environment, naturally place their nose to the ground.

Smelling the ground will send messages to their brain, activating the bowel and bladder.

If after 5 minutes your dog shows no interest in relieving, take them back inside, monitor their movements and then take them out about an hour later, unless you notice they are fidgety.

If an accident happens in the house, do not scold your dog off. Whether in the moment or after the fact.

In the moment, you will bring a negative association with their action of peeing/pooing and they will hesitate to relieve when outside with you. This will lead to them finding a quiet place in the house when you are not looking.

After the fact they will just see you as angry and upset, which may cause them to be wary of you. There will be no association of their relieving to your upset demeanour.

If you do these actions, you will break any level of trust that has started to develop with you.

Relief routine

These are the important times to take your dog out to relieve.

First thing in the morning after you get out of bed.

Before breakfast and 1 hour after they have eaten.

Every 2 hours after that if you are at home or you are establishing a routine.

Playing will activate the bowel and bladder, so if you are playing inside, take them out after a few minutes of interaction. They will usually relieve themselves at this point.

Before their evening meal.

1 hour after eating.

Before bed time.

A Cautionary Tale – Bloat

Bloat is a condition that happens if a dog is exercised too soon after eating (or drinking a large volume of water). It is where the stomach, being full with food, will start to twist. Air and gases are trapped and the stomach will start to expand rapidly. This puts pressure on the heart and lungs. You have to take your dog to the vet immediately as this condition happens quickly and is fatal. Veterinary attention is required urgently for survival. Ref:2

Always, always, allow at least two hours after a meal before exercising. And an hour after exercise before feeding.

Walking/relieving

Give your dog a chance to relieve before their walk and when you return to your home.

Why?

This adds to their relief routine and they will be able to enjoy their time with you when out and about. And because deciding you want to walk your dog for exercise, have fun and enjoy the one-on-one time with them. They will also be more attentive when their bladder and bowels are empty, they will be less distracted and when in the future you are doing training sessions with them, they will be able to focus on what you want.

Or.... if you just want to wander and allow your dog to sniff every post and pee wherever they want, that's fine too. But remember that if after some time you want them to walk at heel with you, it may become a difficult task to establish.

Dogs naturally use their nose to gain information from the environment. Lowering the head and sniffing the ground can be two things. One, they are checking for pee-mail (information from other dogs that have been there before) and two, they are also giving one of many calming signals.

For dogs that have had no guidance for a routine, they will take longer to become established. Be patient with them and yourself. It may take a week or two. Expect accidents to happen and when they do, chill…it is not your dog's fault.

Observing your dog, is helping you to know your dog.

Shelter

With a roof over their head, a place for a comfortable bed is a must!

Placing their bed in a quiet area, safe from intrusion, will allow your dog to rest peacefully, sleep comfortably and feel safe.

Place the bed in a corner, away from foot traffic, the TV, speakers, direct sunlight and other intrusions.

Their shelter must be cool in the summer and warm in the winter.

The dog's bed is a place where, once the dog is on his bed, he should not be disturbed. It is his safety place. All humans, whether small or tall, family or visitors need to know and respect the dog when in their bed. It is your dog's place to go for timeout from the rest of the house. Do not call the dog off, lure, or entice off the bed. And most importantly, do not keep going to check on them by peering around the corner.

Why?

Your dog needs to know that when they are tired or do not want to interact with anyone, they can go and know they will not be disturbed. They can relax and most importantly, they will start to feel safe with you.

Wash bedding every couple of weeks. You will lessen the dog smells.

Toys and chews can be kept in a toy box, with access for your dog to go and choose what they want.

If your dog takes a toy or chew to their bed, you do not take it from them. Remember their bed is their sanctuary.

Sleep

'Sleep is where the brain processes experiences from the day for a fresh start tomorrow'

Sleep is so important. This is when the body regenerates, heals and processes learning experiences from the day.

As your dog becomes comfortable and starts to feel safe within their home environment and you, they will begin to have restful sleep.

Dogs naturally nap throughout their day. That is in their makeup, that is who they are as a species. They nap after playtimes, walks and when you leave the house. They nap after they have eaten. This is an important aspect to aid digestion. Remember a healthy gut is a healthy dog!

When your dog has been with you for a week or so and if you are teaching them new things, training or going to new environments, allow them to nap afterwards. It will help with processing the new information.

If you are training them to do something specific, keep lessons short. If they are not understanding what you want, don't get frustrated, have a playtime and then let them nap.

Willow example

Willow's need to keep herself busy and keep moving was a part of her anxiety, amplified by her energy and playfulness. Not being able to nap peacefully throughout the day added to this high activity rate in her brain.

Giving her some new skills in showing her that it was okay to go on her bed and not do anything but rest or chew her toy, did take a few weeks. Consistently showing her what to do and bringing in the word "Settle" when she did so.

As she progressed with this, over several weeks, she started to take herself to the bed and take naps. I noticed her anxiety lessened but she would still get over excited with people or dogs who visited or who we met on the street. This was all part of the process of getting to know her and having a plan on how to develop her coping strategies.

Sleeping on your bed.

If your dog is new to you, it is best not to let them sleep on the bed, initially.

Why?

Firstly, they will not have a restful sleep with your movement waking them during the night, which may lead them to become a bit grumbly. They need their restful sleep, as well as you.

If they do jump on the bed, before you want them to, lure them off with a toy or throw a bit of kibble on the floor, so they move off the bed on their own. Avoid moving them off with your hand or forcing them off. They may react negatively. Avoid the confrontation. Remember, this is all new to them and they have no reason to trust you yet.

Teaching them in different situations around the home, the "Off" and "Wait", will bring in listening skills, self-control and healthy, vocal responses to you.

Certainly, after a month or so, you can invite them onto your bed in the morning for a cuddle. Once you know each other better and your dog is learning to ask with your help.

Place their bed near to your bed, put their favourite toy with them and as they step on their bed you can say "In your bed" to reinforce what you are asking them to do.

The effects of trauma on restful sleep.

It is important to know that if your dog has been through a trauma of any kind, restful sleep is paramount in their healing process.

Maintaining consistency with all of their needs, will over time help them feel safer, so that they will start to gain more restful sleep.

Why?

In a 'trauma' state, the brain is on high alert and is conditioned to keep the body safe. Processing of information through all the senses, especially the eyes and ears can be overwhelming.

Information from the environment is processed but not filtered as to what is and what is not important. So everything seen, heard and felt is a potential threat to the safety of the dog. This is overwhelming for the dog not only mentally but physically as well.

The dog will be reactive to movement, noise and touch and will always be looking for a safe place to retreat to.

Processing of information from the environment is taken in however the brain cannot filter what it needs to, to feel safe, so everything becomes a threat.

The dog will react in either of two ways, dependant on what has worked or not worked before. He will lash out, with or without warning or go quiet and 'shutdown'.

Either way, their need for feeling safe is your responsibility in that moment. Showing the dog where they can be in a safe place to sleep regularly and routinely, will help the brain be in a healthier state for functioning and processing information. This allows them the ability to start to cope and take in their surroundings, with your help and guidance.

Safety Needs

"Safety gives a platform on which your dog can start to explore with you"

Consistency, Patience & Compassion

Routines for all of us in our daily lives, ensure we can maintain a surviving life to give us the platform on which we can start to explore and thrive.

Consistency, Patience and Compassion as a dog handler or owner, starts with developing routines and guidelines on a daily basis for your dog.

Your dog needs to know your home is a safe place. Showing them takes time. Depending on who your dog is, will depend on how long it will take.

Home, where their life needs are being consistently and successfully met, will start to feel safe for them.

Your consistency, patience and compassion in understanding what they need to feel safe, will go a long way in their success with the other needs on the steps of the ladder to a successful, thriving life.

Once your dog feels safe in the environments you initially take them, then the small steps of learning will start to take place with you.

The questions that need to be answered are: Is your home a safe place? Are the outer doors closed so no escape is possible? Is the yard safe to go into or have you a quiet place for them to relieve? Is there a place to free run in an enclosed area? No mixing with strange dogs you meet on the street, until you and your dog know each other. How is the recall progressing?

Safety starts in the home with you. How you are feeling with your 'safe place' will transmit to your dog. They will learn by your posture, demeanour and how you interact and speak to other people, as to who you are. Your delightful pheromones give away your emotional state, which the dog, with its exceptional sense of smell and observation skills, will recognize and start to associate with your body language.

New Environments

Safety extends into each environment you take your dog into. Whether going for their first or subsequent walks, going for a run, meeting new people, seeing new dogs/animals, new sights and sounds, traffic, moving objects like skateboards and bikes, (which are always frightening), garbage bins and the new smells.

All of these will have an impact on your dog, whether a puppy or a grown dog.

Their experiences and how they have had to deal with similar situations before will also have an impact on how they are feeling in the situation.

If your dog does not feel safe they will let you know by how they react or act upon situations.

If you have been successful with the life needs, your dog will look to you for support in these situations. If your support is not forthcoming – they will look after themselves, in the only way they can, by instinctive and learnt behaviour. This will be seen as a bark, growl, lunging, shying or backing away, low body demeanour, trying to run away, peeing (fear based), pulling on the leash, jumping up on you or people passing by or objects, biting the leash, picking up objects to carry, mouthing or nipping at you.

All behaviours that are a clear indication of "I am scared!" "I do not know what to do", "I want to run away, but cannot", "I have to defend myself, to keep me safe". All avoidance behaviours.

So many of these responses can be seen in lesser or greater degrees, dependant on whether you have fulfilled the life needs in your home and you are observing their language and getting to know them better.

The question you need to ask yourself is "Has my dog started to feel safe with me?"

If your dog responds with concern to the environment they are in at the time, an object, person or another dog, then take them away from the concern, back to where they were successful. This may even be going back home.

Interacting with them with your voice, saying to them calmly, "You are awesome" and everything is OK. At the same time, walking back the way you came and even heading for home, the safe place, will be having an impact on their relationship with you. You have heard what they are saying in their body language and you are taking them to safety.

This is a step towards trust.

Many fears and concerns can be avoided by taking small steps. For example: the first walk should be down your street (or in a quiet area), no more than 50 metres, then return home. It may take 10 minutes it may take more, the important thing to remember is your dog is exploring with eyes, ears, nose, touch and taste, this new environment you are taking them into.

This is a great opportunity to observe your dog, see how they respond to what is around them. Talk to them occasionally, if they look up at you, acknowledge by looking back softly and telling them they are doing a good job. Are they sniffing, looking about or walking close to you? Are they walking out in front or walking behind? What is the tail, head, ears and general gait and demeanour telling you? Relaxed or stiff jointed? Do they look light in their movement or are they moving with a heaviness about them?

Allow them room to move on the leash, so keep it loose. Initially, do not ask for or expect any obedience because it is not going to happen!

Observe, Observe, Observe. This is where you see the real dog in new environments. And your dog is assessing you too!

You will learn so much from them in this short walk. If you acknowledge what they can and cannot do, this will lead into a greater understanding as to what they need from you to be as successful as they can be.

Security

Your dog needs to feel safe and know they are safe. The home is the starting point for your relationship to develop. Establishing life needs of food, water, relieving, warmth, bed, shelter and sleep is the place to start feeling safe and cared for.

You will notice as they begin to feel more comfortable they will give you more eye contact, they will come up for some nice contact and maybe a bum rub. When you see this happening, you are giving your dog choice in coming to you because they want to, not because you have asked them too. This is success.

When your dog has the freedom to choose, then they are more open and readier to start learning.

Willow started to show signs that she was feeling safe with me when she eventually went to sleep that first night. Her behaviour in the morning with placing her head on the bed and waiting for me to open my eyes and greet her, was an indication that she was starting to feel comfortable enough to place her head not far from mine.

Providing a safe home, supporting them by showing what you want them to achieve, are the keys to your dog feeling comfortable and safe with you. This is an enormous step in your relationship.

Your voice is so influential in maintaining their security with you. Calm, yet assertive (without volume), when danger may be nearby. Telling them "Everything is good" is letting them know you are looking after them. A sideward glance with soft eyes accompanied by a sideways stance, is a calming signal to your dog.

If you think about the first time human meet, the actions of shaking hands is brought about by extending your right arm and hand diagonally across your body, some eye contact, giving a softer and more welcoming approach. How do you feel when the person you shake hands with mirrors your body language? How do you feel if they are more abrupt, more head on, take a firmer grip and maintain an eye contact? Makes you uncomfortable? Do you retreat back to your 'safe space' or do you stand your ground?

Critical Area or Safe Space

This is an immediate comfort space around your dog. You have it too as I am sure you are aware. It becomes more noticeable for you in crowded situations. On a bus, in the line at the grocery store, etc. How do you feel when another person steps into your space or faces you directly? Do you stand your ground to see how they respond, or do you move away slightly so you can maintain your space?

The comfort space for your dog may be large or small. Your dog will let you know. If a dog is approached and they feel threatened or violated in or near their space they will likely react defensively with barking, growling or they will avoid and show shyness and fear.

Initial Greetings

Always, always allow the dog to approach you first. Invite with your body language. Acknowledge them with a soft sideways glance & a sideways stance. If they do not want to engage, do not take it personally.

When you invite your dog to you and they approach and allow you to stroke them, (gently and slowly on the side of their shoulder, not the top of the head), this is by their choice. This is so healthy, and you are building up trust.

Allowing them to make the choice to approach you first whether it is the first meeting or the hundredth, it will give them the choice to make the decision based on how they are feeling – at the time.

What is going on in the environment at the time and how your body language is viewed by the dog, will indicate whether you are safe to approach or not.

Order

Any successful community, family or establishment has an order within it for feeling safe and knowing what is coming up next. This is essential to survive and grow. Even though there may be a busyness to your life, your dog knowing the routines and guidelines on a daily basis - the order of things – will help them settle, be comfortable and relax in their environment.

How the day unfolds is dependent on what is happening in the environment at that time. It may seem chaotic or busy but underneath, the routines and guidelines are the same.

Chaos theory: which simply means that even though the surface implies chaos, deep within the chaos there is order.

Limits and Guidelines

Limits are the boundaries of where your dog can and cannot go within the home environment and when they are with you in the outside environment.

Guidelines are you showing the dog these limits and you maintaining the consistency in showing these limits.

When Willow came to my home, I kept her on leash and went with her to explore the apartment. This was to help her remain calm and not run around at great speed and hurt herself. Showing her where she had access to water and where her bed was and of course where the toys and bones were was the starting point for the guidelines in my home.

Introductions for new dogs to family and resident dogs

No parties for your new arrival. Your dog needs to see your home as a safe place and have the space it needs to adjust to their new home.

People introductions should be quiet and with the dog approaching them, not the other way around. People should stand slightly sideways, no continual eye contact, just a soft look Remember, sideways stance with a sideways glance. And no contact.

Allow the dog to approach the family members if they want to. Do not overly fuss. Say a nice calm hello, let them sniff if they want to, then let them explore the rest of the house and garden – all the time on a loose leash.

Dogs love to smell feet, legs and the crotch area. When they go to smell any of these areas, calmly turn slightly sideways and when they go to the crotch area, turn away calmly.

Keep your voice and body language calm while you are taking them through the house to see all the places they will be allowed to go. Show them the water bowl and where you have prepared a bed in a room for them.

If you already have a resident dog the best way to introduce them is outside on neutral ground, like the street (if safe) or somewhere quiet. It is best to have room to go for a walk together (just a hundred metres or so) and a place where they will likely pee!

Keeping both dogs on a loose leash allowing them to sniff (usually butts) for 5 seconds then call the resident dog away, to give space to both dogs. Do this several times until the dogs sniff the ground and look away from each other. Then go for a quiet walk, both dogs in line with each other, allow sniffing but keep a healthy distance away. Then as you return home, gradually merge nearer, still giving both dogs space.

When going into the house take the new dog in first, still keep the resident dog at a healthy distance, then explore the house together on leashes. Show him where the water bowl is as he may want a drink. They may both want a drink but allow them space around the water bowl so they can drink individually.

Remember to give room for both dogs (critical area) and let them know they are doing an awesome job, calmly.

The Why's to this way of introduction is to avoid confrontation for everyone. The last thing the new dog needs is to be restricted in having a choice to see what is going on and sniffing the environment.

You are also setting precedent for giving out the guidelines.

When you have finished exploring the house settle down, have a cup of tea or just sit quietly and allow the new dog to settle with you. (Still on leash).

When the dog offers to sit or lies down, bring in the word you want to use (as sit or down) when the dog is doing the action.

Then "Good Job……..Settle" all the while you are relaxed and just observing the new dog.

You are starting to bring in what you want the dog to do, but when they are comfortable. No force is necessary to get the dog to do a certain action.

Why? Because they are not going to respond to you, as they do not know you. And the word and intonation you use may be different or new from previously learned. When you bring in a word for the action you require, over time the dog will respond much quicker as he had some choice initially.

After 20 minutes or so, when you feel the dog is a bit more relaxed, let him off leash quietly while you are sitting together. Observe him, allow him the room to explore, show him the bed and the toy box. If you have another dog, let the new dog off leash first, then the resident dog. No toys at this point, as this may cause an argument. Remember, they are your toys.

Observe both dogs and make sure they are comfortable together and responding to their names when and if you call them.

Acknowledging the dogs individually will avoid jealousy starting to arise. When you acknowledge one dog for anything, acknowledge the other dog also by name. As an example, if dog A is barking and you ask him to "Quiet" and he does, "Quiet...Good Boy - A". Then look at dog B and tell them they are awesome too, using their name. This is the start of supporting and being aware of your dogs.

Feeding

When it is feed time, feed them separately in different rooms. Why? Because the new dog needs to know the feed routine and you do not want any food altercations with them both.

Food is a basic need and for a new dog this is a high stakes survival need. Watching the new dog eat will give an indication of how he eats. Is he quick? Does he gobble? Is he a slow eater? These are indications of how he is feeling about food. As the days go by he may start to relax. If he gobbles place a Kong or bone in his bowl. This will slow him down and give him a chance to lick his bowl and slow down/calm his mouth action.

After a few weeks you could feed them in the same room, as they both know the procedure. Keep the bowls a good distance away from each other. If one dog is more food oriented, place a leash on him before you feed him to keep him away from the other dog when he finishes. Ask him to sit and wait, while you support him with the leash. Remember to ask both of them to sit and wait when they finish eating. Then pick up the bowls and release them from their sit. This will avoid any opportunity for food possessiveness.

Not Eating

When a dog goes into a new environment or situation, the nervous and sensory systems are on high alert for any dangers to their own well-being. One of these responses is for the digestive system to shutdown, which is part of the flight or fight response. A dog will not be able to eat if they feel unsafe. It is all part of the stress response, to make sure all the blood supply goes to the vital organs to keep them working, until the 'threat' goes away.

When your new dog seems uninterested in food, they could be in this state. You need to ask yourself these questions:

How much water is my dog drinking? When stressed, dogs will drink more to keep hydrated. It is an automatic response. (So you need to take them out to relieve more often). Dogs will eat better if their bladder and bowels are empty.

Is it excessive or do they drink very little? This is a sign of anxiety. Make sure the water is clean and freshened at least twice a day.

Is the food good and does it smell fresh? With a good quality food, you will smell the freshness. Stress and anxiety in new environments, situations or routines will affect the dog's ability to eat.

Am I giving my dog too much food in the bowl at one time? Overwhelming the dog by giving too much will in fact turn a dog away (more so if they are a naturally sensitive eater).

Is the dog eating treats? Does he snatch the treat or take it gently? These are indications of the stress levels of your dog. If you are scolding the dog for snatching and then withdrawing the treat, they may associate that with their meal and will be reluctant to eat. Do not give treats at this stage.

Is the feeding/eating area quiet for my dog to eat in peace? Ensure your dog has his own space for meal times.

If your dog has a dry mouth or over salivates this is a sign of stress. I am simplifying things here, because if your dog is one of the breeds that salivates a lot, then this could be 'normal' for them. This is what you have to find out by going through the basic needs.

Not eating can cause you anxiety, as all you want is for the dog to have a meal. If your dog goes to the bowl and turns away uninterested, rather than try and entice the dog to eat by drawing attention to the bowl or feeding them out of your hand, just pick up the bowl, make no fuss, and offer it again 30 minutes later. Do not get overly worried, unless you think it may be a health issue, then take your dog to your vet.

Also think about does my dog need to relieve? Do they need to poo? Emptying the bowel and bladder before eating will allow the digestive system to replenish with a new meal. If your dog has not fully recovered or rested after exercise, playing or out walking, then this can contribute to your dog not eating. Remember, no exercise one hour before or two hours after eating. Being in a calm state will give your dog a chance to eat healthily.

Jane E Madigan

Belonging

**"Healthy relationships within your family, will
fulfill the need to belong"**

Loving and fussing your dog before the basic needs
are established can lead to dysfunction and
challenges. This could be perceived as having a
problem dog with behaviour issues.

This is all too often the mistake that happens. And
most of the time it is not seen until 2-4 weeks into
the dog being in a new home. I often hear this
saying "a new dog will have a honeymoon period
of about 2 weeks, where the dog will pretty much
behave. After this time, the dog's true colours will
start to shine." In those weeks the dog is figuring
you out, trying to understand the routines and your
body language and voice.

If their need for routine and feeling safe are not
met, then their behaviour is going to show through
in many different ways. Examples of this are

anxiety, not wanting to be touched, separation anxiety, unsettled (fidgety), protectiveness, relieving issues in the house, wanting to be near you and at the same time not wanting to be touched. Suddenly reactive to things, which you never saw before. One or more of these behaviours will appear.

Yes, we can show love and give our dog cuddles, when your dog is ready for this from you. This will happen when a huge level of trust and feeling safe has been attained and maintained. It is the same for any relationship we venture into. We have to trust and feel safe with somebody before we let them near us. Not only does it take time to build these feelings but during this time they are getting to know you too. It's a two-way process and the same applies to a person and their dog.

It is natural in all family and social groups. Showing affection comes after trust and safety have started to be established and maintained within the other needs being met.

Getting to know one another is all about observing body language, watching how things are done, even where the water bowl is and what time the food arrives. Actions and words spoken and your intonation with body language will all be deciphered by your dog. Remember they know dog language. Human body language is different and complex. So are voices. They have to learn it by watching and listening to you. How do you think you are doing with your impression?

Building trust takes time. Breaking your dog's trust can happen in an instant.

It takes time to get to know someone. The actions and words another human speaks to you will go towards the building up of rapport, feeling safe and starting to trust the person. Intonation of their words that they speak, demeanour, behaviour and touch and being consistent in how they interact with you and with others, to even how safe you feel when you are being driven in a car with them, all add to trust and safety being built, respectfully.

So when your new dog comes into your life, no matter their age or history, how you are with them, showing the rules and guidelines are the most important things you can do, to start the feeling of belonging, whether it is just you, a family or other members in the house.

Your dog will be looking to see who does what and how the group responds in situations. The group/family dynamic is about fitting in. There should be one person who will do everything for the dog, initially. That person will care for and show the dog what they need to do. Relieving, feeding, walking, etc. It is all about the dog learning to be consistently successful in understanding the routines and guidelines, from that one person, so no signals are misinterpreted or misunderstood. (We may think that we do things the same, but we do not).

Once your dog is established in the routines (maybe a few weeks in their new environment) then you can show other family members what you do, but more importantly what habits the dog has and his body language. Everyone must be consistent and watch the dog, sideways stance and a sideways glance.

Affection is a two-way process and is about being included in everyday activities and routines. Being spoken to, learning to play and have fun are important not only for your dog but you as well. This is when you really start to get to know each other. Allow your dog to be a dog and do dog things. Find out what makes them happy!

Willow

When Willow was living in kennels at the training centre, she began to settle into the routines, having other dogs to mix and play with and got to know the staff who looked after her. This took a week or so for her to start to look comfortable. Her need for belonging was fulfilled by where she was living most of the time. On the weekends, Willow came home with me, so her need for belonging when she was with me was fulfilled. Having two places where this need was met, helped her move forward with becoming who she was.

Jane E Madigan

Achievement

"Success is the sum of small efforts repeated day in and day out"

Robert Collier

Feeling Good

Feeling good about oneself is a clear indication that all is right in your world, in this moment. What has led up to feeling good is dependent on the life, safety and belonging needs being fulfilled, knowing you are comfortable with friends whom you feel safe with, the environment you are in and how your whole day is going for you.

Achieving a task or working towards a successful outcome makes you feel so good, more so when someone else acknowledges your success and congratulates you on a job well done!

With these successes, your confidence and overall feeling good grows into other areas of your life.

Your whole life opens up to a healthier attitude of having choices to exploring, problem solving, approaching and learning new things. Your demeanour will be relaxed, you may be a bit cheeky and start telling jokes. Your true character will start to show up and you will feel good about life in general.

It is the same for your dog.

When your dog feels good, you will see them start to initiate play, come to you for interaction on their own, respond to you when you call their name. Their eating will be healthy as they will eat all their food at meal times so their digestive system will be working well.

Their poo, yes, we always come back to how well they poo with regularity, the consistency of it and how much they actually poo compared to their size!

They will be less inclined to follow you everywhere. They will see you go to the bathroom and decide not to follow you (or they may decide that you need to be monitored, like you monitor them when they go)! As you enter or leave a room, they will likely just look up at you from where they are, or they will check to see if you are going anywhere interesting!

They will be content to hang out with you, be less clingy and more relaxed and chill.

All this happens because they know the routines and guidelines, they are starting to understand what type of person you are and what you are likely to do. And, when you call and invite them to you, they are more likely to come to you straight away, as they know the nice touch you will give them.

You will notice they will respond to you when out walking. You will be able to take them further from home without them feeling overwhelmed by the environment.

They are responding to the words you have consistently used when a behaviour has been offered. Now they are at the point where you can ask for a 'sit' or 'stand', 'wait' or 'heel' they are more likely to be successful!! Yes, it is all coming together!

Willow

When I adopted Willow, taking her to any new environment always made her anxious and highly stressed. Keeping the same routes short for many weeks as we got to know each other better, helped with reducing her anxiety levels.

I was not going to change who, in essence she was however, I was able to recognize when she was likely going into this 'state' before it exasperated into full blown anxiety.

We did reverse routes, which started as no more than 20 metres, letting her have a sniff and pee if she wanted to, then turning around and going back home. This worked well for her. On the return she was able to listen to me better, I could start to teach her some things, and we could have some fun. She would also look up at me more but the biggest thing I noticed about her is that her gait became more relaxed and her tail would swing in time with her body, in a relaxed and natural fashion.

We would do this same route 3 times a day. Each time we went out, I took her an extra metre or two. After about a week we did a short block route. Then I took her from home down to the river where there was a bench. I would sit and give her the 7ft of the loose leash to move around. She would explore and when she offered a sit or down, I would bring in the word as she was going through the action. Then we would hang out for a while and we could both watch the world go by.

As she progressed over the weeks, I would take her out in the car to parks during the quiet times of the day with not too much going on and find a bench and relax. She loved doing this. And then she got into the habit of picking up a soft toy when leaving the house, so we could take it with us and she would carry it if and when she needed it.

These opportunities of observing gave me insights into Willow and how I could help her better. As she progressed, we then ventured into doing more together.

Voice intonation was key in Willow's progress. A calm voice, no matter how she was feeling, was instrumental in helping Willow to evolve. Talking to her in a calm, normal voice, telling her she was doing awesome and everything was fine, was how she started to have trust in that I was looking after her and keeping her safe.

As well as bringing in a word for the behaviour she offered, how I said it was just as important. As I have said, being calm in my voice without sounding too quiet so she knew I was supporting her, was instrumental in her understanding that what she was doing was right.

My body language along with my voice showed her how I was feeling. Voice and body language go together, and this is what your dog sees and hears and makes the associations with. Remaining in a calm and relaxed manner and being seen as self-assured (even when sometimes I may not have been feeling that way) was what she needed at this time and consequently throughout her life.

Learning

"When your dog is in a mentally and physically calm state, they will be open to a deeper learning, at an accelerated rate"

Teaching and showing your dog what you want them to achieve is about being relaxed, having fun and the number one 'must' for all dog owners is having a sense of humour and being able to laugh at yourself when things do not go according to plan.

It does not matter what other people think, it is about you and your dog having a healthy, respectful and fun relationship. Your dog deserves this from you.

New Learning

Are you mentally and physically comfortable?

For you to learn and be taught a new task successfully, what do you need to achieve success?

When you start to think about how you learned your skill set, was it in a noisy, busy and new environment? How did you feel? Did it take you a while to grasp what was wanted of you? Was the person showing and training you good at what they did, were they patient and understanding of your needs to learn successfully or did they show you once and leave you to figure it out on your own? Did they tell you when you were doing great or tell you, you were doing it wrong? How did you feel? Even after grasping the concept, how was your self-esteem? Did you feel confident about your new skill? When did it become a responsive skill?

You can relate all of this to how your dog feels also.

My Learning

Back in the late 80's, when I went from working with horses into working with computers, I was learning a totally new skill. Computers were big mainframes, noisy modems and very loud business printers, all in an air-conditioned room!

Being taught the keyboard skills to monitor these business machines, how to correctly load the big reel of tape to do the backups and learning how they worked and integrated with each other, was a scary process for me. I had never done anything like this before. In the early days I was totally out of my depth, feeling overwhelmed and wondering if I had done the right thing.

The one person who believed I could do the job was the chief operator. His patience in showing me the basics and making sure I was successful with them before showing me more tasks and how they all worked with each other, and to ensure the smooth running of the business, was invaluable for my successful outcome. This allowed me to gain confidence with my new skill set and feel comfortable to know I could ask him questions, if I was still unsure. When there was an issue with any of the computers or machines, my new confidence allowed me to problem solve and make decisions through my choices, to be successful.

Your Dog's learning

Your dog needs the patience, time and space to see and hear what you are teaching (just like I did back in the late 80's). This is more successful for your dog, when you start from a place of them feeling safe with you and the environment they are in.

Your dog will learn more successfully and more quickly when their mind and body are relaxed.

They always do and they always will.

Reaching this state, by giving them the basic needs for survival, and allowing them the time to get to know you and you to know them, enables them to listen and watch you more easily.

When you want to teach them something, have in your mind what you would like them to achieve, then break it down into baby steps. This way they will learn what you want quickly and then if they are not understanding you, take them back a step to where they were last successful. If he is not understanding, you may need to assess and change how you are teaching it.

An example of teaching baby steps to reach an objective: Guide dog kerb work

When training guide dogs to stop at a down kerb, you have to teach the sit or stand first. I initially would teach a solid stand. How would I do this? In baby steps and in a safe and comfortable environment for the dog (Not out on the street where he would be eventually making the association with the kerb and the stand). When the dog, whose name is Malt, would stand naturally when he was with me, on leash, I would bring in the word "Stand' as he stood still. I would also be teaching the "Steady" when walking about the training centre on leash, so he would slow his walking and then I could help him achieve a stand. (I would also teach a speed up command too ... "Hup, Upp").

As he started to understand what was being asked which happened very quickly with Malt, as he was a bright boy, I would be walking along and ask for "Steadeeee", along with the ease and feel of the leash. He would then slow his pace and I would match my pace to his, and then bring in "Ssstttand" with easing and feeling of the leash and stepping up towards his shoulder and turning towards him, so as to help him stand in balance. As he stood, I would repeat "Stand, good boy". (All of this was without treats) When we did these types of short exercises, I would have a toy (Splatt, the little teddy bear) in my pocket and Malt and I would go and have a play for a few minutes, or I would give him some free time in the grass run (that we had at the centre). Always playing after lesson time, whether a success or not, is so important for the dog and also for me, to release energy and stress. This is building up a fun relationship.

Once Malt was able to respond to just my voice and be successful at standing on his own, I then worked him to the kerbs at the centre. (This all being a familiar and safe place for him to learn successfully). Once he had accomplished responding to my voice and had started to make a connection with the stand and stopping at the presence of a kerb, I then took him into a quiet neighbourhood with kerbs. I was consistent with the commands and body language that he had learned and understood in the quiet and safe area of the centre. We practised the stand a couple of times, before walking towards the down kerb. When I was about 10 feet away and we were walking at a steady pace, I asked for a "Steadeee" Then with 6 feet to go, asked for the "Stand".

This is not boot camp, so I was not expecting Malt to come to an abrupt standstill! Besides, he had 2 back legs that needed to catch up with what was going on with his front legs! And with a new environment brings new distractions of smells, sights and sounds. As soon as he stopped, "Stand, good boy" I gave some quiet touch as praise as well, which was what he had received with all the teachings previously.

After a few seconds of "wait" and I checked there were no moving cars coming towards us, we then moved forward. At each down kerb I approached the same routine was carried out, so he knew what was coming next and he got the vocal support to go along with everything. At this point in his early training, if Malt stepped over any kerb into the road, it was my fault for not preparing him on his approach. Whether my timing was wrong or I was distracted or miscalculated, it was always on me. Taking responsibility for a mistake was my learning curve. It allowed me to think through what I was asking him, whether he understood what I was teaching him, or did I need to change how I was teaching.

These initial sessions were short, we had fun on the sidewalk between the down kerbs. Splatt would often come out of my pocket for Malt to carry. He loved carrying him. He would often carry him for the next few down kerbs, before dropping him on the sidewalk for me to pick up!! All good fun and great for building the relationship.

As Malt progressed through his training and was stopping and standing on his own at the down kerb, he would then sit on his own without prompting. This was when I realized he knew what to do and was confident and comfortable enough with moving traffic. As he sat, I would bring in "Sit, good boy", a nice stroke down the side of his neck, reinforcing what I wanted him to do, but he was doing it all on his own anyway.

Telling you my little story about Malt is about those baby steps.

Working with the small steps of success to reach an objective, where the dog is learning in their time, is so much more empowering for the dog. Your relationship will prosper as trust and safety are being continually built. Your knowledge of your dog and knowing who they are at a deeper level will be strengthened.

A relationship with your dog is about having fun, you being inspired to do right by your dog and empowering your dog to be successful!

Accomplishing the previous basic needs has given you the opportunity to see who they are and how they process their environments.

Work on easily obtained successes, like the sit, down, wait and stay, where bringing in a word associated with the behaviour they are offering has brought you to a more trusting place.

Seeing how your dog learns, does he have good listening skills, is he calm when you are teaching him, all add to your information as to who he is and what he can cope with at the time. And most importantly what support he needs from you.

A Successful Learning State

When you get a new dog, getting to know each other at the same time as building up the trust and them feeling safe with you, is paramount in their success to a thriving life.

There should be no expectations to what they do and do not know. Wipe the slate clean and start afresh. Observe them, see what they know by what they offer when you do ask for something, like a sit. Call them to you, are they responsive to their name?

If you want to train your dog to do a specific skill set and you are not trained to train those skills with your dog, go and get yourself trained first.

Your dog needs the skills to think for itself to achieve a task successfully. When they are using their mental capacity to figure things out, you are helping them to be in a calmer mental state. As they start to respond more quickly and precisely to the word you use, they will be in a place of learning more skills. Their confidence and self-esteem will be building along with self-empowerment.

Willow

One of Willow's favourite games was to take whatever hat I was wearing off my head, after our walk! As I bent down to take her harness off, she would very gently take hold of the hat, pull it very slowly off my head as though she did not want me to notice, then, once clear of the harness, would run off, prize in her mouth and throw it up and catch it on its way down! She never chewed, she just loved to carry and have fun. Yes, she would always bring it back to me and as I took hold of it and said 'thank you' she released it. She would then wait to see where I would put it, before sneaking up to it and sneaking it away again!! She always made me laugh.

As I got to really know Willow and she to know me, whenever I taught her anything new, she always learned very quickly. This happens with any dog I train. Part of the process of relationship is to build up the trust and safety aspect quickly, especially when training a working dog, as I would continually assess them for their potential to do the job.

Part of theses aspects (trust and safety) was to allow the dogs to be themselves, so you could see who they were. Trying to take short cuts by missing some baby steps to the objective, fragment the relationship of trust and the dog feeling safe with you. This will show when the dog is unable to be successful in their learning as they are not in a receptive calm state of thriving but rather surviving and reacting and guessing with what was going on around them and responding to body language. A shallow learning that I see too often.

Two things to think about here...

1. Learn to train without ego

2. There is no short cut to any place worth going.

When you are in the moment with your dog, with no expectations on them or yourself, your observation skills will increase and you will start to see who your dog really is without the labels. With this, your relationship will be built on trust and safety at a deeper level.

The use of treats

Treats - misuse and overuse teaches the dog to respond and do things for the treat rather than for you. Changing when you give the treat, changes how your dog learns. Teach and show the objective with baby steps, voice and touch reward. Once they know what you want with the word associated with the behaviour, then give them the treat for achieving the task. When you start to train this way, the dog will have a deeper understanding of the objective, have increased listening skills and you will have a better and deeper understanding of your dog and become an improved handler.

What I have learned and continue to learn

With over twenty years of experience that I have gained working with over a thousand dogs, this is what I know:

Be authentic. This is a two-way process. Take time at the beginning to get to know your dog without expectations. Listen to what they have to say. Teach them whatever you want them to know. Be kind. Be compassionate and be patient with yourself.

A dog steps into your life for a reason. See what they can teach you. And most importantly, have fun together because that is what life is about.

Go and enjoy all those wonderful moments with your best friend.

We all deserve a dog to love and guide us,

Jane

Jane E Madigan

Notes and references

Ref 1: Brain music - marciahoeck.com

Ref 2: Bloat in Dogs – akc.org

About the Author

Jane Madigan is an empathetic and science-based dog consultant specializing in canine behaviours.

Dedicated to helping dogs be all they can be, Jane's expertise enables her to bring a dog to a state of calm, thereby improving listening skills, mobility and accelerated learning so that behavioural issues can be addressed and resolved.

Knowing that the connection and influence of the three aspects of mental, physical and emotional balance is key to a dog being successful as a Companion, Working, Agility, Search and Rescue or Competitive dog, Jane quickly assesses what a dog is experiencing. Using positive approaches of various techniques, she helps the dog achieve this balance.

The dogs Jane works with experience enhanced self-confidence, awareness, carriage, balance, agility, mobility and initiative. These, in turn, contribute positively to a dog's outlook on their world, improved behaviour, ease of movement and successful learning.

Jane has accumulated over 30 years of expertise empowering horses and dogs to reach their full potential including 12 years working with competition horses and 20 years training Guide Dogs for the visually impaired.

Jane's website provides more information: www.inspiredk9s.ca

You can also follow Jane on Facebook, Twitter and Instagram: @inspiredk9s

Inspiring You to Empower Your Dog to Reach Their Full Potential

'We cannot change the essence of who the dog is. However, we can transform them into being the best of themselves' Jane E Madigan

<u>Notes</u>

<u>Notes</u>

Made in the USA
Middletown, DE
21 March 2021

35181456R00062